CAPUCHIN MONKEYS AS PETS

A COMPLETE GUIDE TO CAPUCHIN MONKEYS OWNERSHIP, PROS, CONS, CONSIDERATIONS, DIETS, HEALTH, HABITAT, BEHAVIOR ETC

DR MORRIS HART

Table of Contents

Overview of Capuchin Monkeys

Capuchin monkeys, which belong to the genus Cebus, are small New World primates native to Central and South America. These intelligent and agile creatures, known for their unusual hair tufts like a Capuchin monk's cowl, have piqued humans' interest and intrigue for generations. Their native habitats include a wide range of environments, from rainforests to dry forests, demonstrating flexibility and resilience. Capuchin monkeys typically weigh 3 to 9 pounds and stand 12 to 22 inches tall. They have a variety of fur colors, including brown, black, and white.

Capuchin monkeys are gregarious primates that live in groups of 10 to 30 individuals, each led by a dominant male. These groups are distinguished by intricate social structures and interactions, in which grooming, play, and communication via vocalizations and facial expressions play critical roles in sustaining group cohesiveness. Capuchin monkeys are noted for their amazing intellect in the wild, where they are frequently seen foraging for food with tools, breaking nuts with stones, and extracting insects from crevices. Their food is omnivorous, including fruits, nuts, seeds, insects, small vertebrates, and bird eggs.

One of the most appealing characteristics of Capuchin monkeys is their cognitive ability. Studies have demonstrated that they have superior problem-solving abilities, a good memory, and the ability to learn by observation and imitation. This intellect, combined with their lively and curious temperament, has piqued the curiosity of researchers as well as pet owners. However, their complicated demands and behaviors present considerable obstacles for pet owners, so understanding their natural history and requirements is critical for anybody thinking about bringing a Capuchin monkey into their house.

- Popularity as Pets

The temptation of owning a Capuchin monkey as a pet has been fostered by a variety of factors, including its appealing looks, presumed intellect, and portrayal in media and entertainment. Capuchin monkeys have appeared in various films, television series, and commercials, where they are frequently portrayed as naughty yet loving companions. This media exposure has greatly increased their popularity among exotic pet enthusiasts.

However, the practice of keeping Capuchin monkeys as pets is not a new phenomena. Historically, indigenous peoples preserved these primates, followed by European explorers who came upon them on their travels. Capuchin monkeys rose to prominence in the United States throughout the twentieth century, when they were frequently seen performing in circuses and sideshows. This historical context has impacted contemporary perceptions of Capuchin monkeys as fascinating and engaging companions.

Despite their growing popularity, keeping a Capuchin monkey as a pet presents several problems and ethical considerations. Capuchin monkeys, unlike traditional pets like dogs and cats, have complex social, psychological, and physical demands that can be challenging to manage in a home setting. Prospective owners must evaluate their long-term commitment, as Capuchin monkeys can live up to 40 years in captivity. This longevity necessitates a consistent investment of time, money, and resources to preserve their health.

The growing demand for Capuchin monkeys as pets has sparked concerns about the impact on wild populations and the possibility of criminal commerce. Capturing wild Capuchin monkeys for the pet trade can cause large losses in their natural populations and upset the ecological balance of their environments. Furthermore, the act of catching and transporting these creatures is typically brutal, resulting in high mortality and suffering.

As the discussion over the suitability of Capuchin monkeys as pets continues, it is critical to thoroughly consider the pros and negatives. On the one hand, their brains and engaging personalities make them interesting companions. However, the problems of supporting their needs, as well as the ethical considerations of keeping a wild animal in captivity, must not be overlooked. Understanding the complexities of owning Capuchin monkeys is the first step toward making an informed and responsible decision.

Overview of Capuchin Monkeys

- Natural Habitat and Distribution

Capuchin monkeys are found in a variety of environments throughout Central and South America. They live in Brazil, Colombia, Venezuela, Honduras, and Costa Rica, and thrive in a variety of habitats ranging from tropical rainforests to dry deciduous forests and mangroves. This adaptability to varied ecosystems demonstrates their resilience and versatility. Capuchin monkeys cross the rainforest's dense canopy with incredible agility, relying on their prehensile tails for stability and balance. These monkeys are arboreal, spending the most of their time in trees, where they can obtain food, shelter, and protection from predators.

In their natural habitat, Capuchin monkeys play an important ecological role. They act as seed dispersers, dispersing seeds through their feces to help forests regenerate themselves. Their foraging activity also has an impact on the distribution of diverse plant species, which in turn influences the structure and composition of ecosystems. Capuchin monkeys also serve as prey for larger predators like jaguars and birds of prey, making them an important element of the food chain.

- Physical characteristics

Capuchin monkeys are small to medium-sized primates with particular morphological characteristics. They have a round head, an expressive face, and wide eyes that show a variety of moods. Their limbs are robust and flexible, so they can move quickly through the woods. The prehensile tail, which can grasp and hold objects, distinguishes them from many other ape species. This tail adds an extra limb for balance and mobility, which improves their arboreal existence.

Capuchin monkeys' fur varies in color, with distinct species showing colors of brown, black, white, and gold. The most well-known species, the white-faced Capuchin (Cebus capucinus), has a prominent white face and throat that contrast with its dark body fur. Another species, the black-capped Capuchin (Cebus apella), has a dark cap of fur on its head. These color variations and patterns aid in the identification of distinct species and subspecies within the genus.

- Social Structure and Behavior

Capuchin monkeys are highly sociable animals who live in groups known as armies. These units are made up of many males, females, and their offspring, with group sizes ranging from ten to thirty. The social organization is hierarchical, with the dominant male at the apex, followed by other males, females, and juveniles. Grooming, play, and vocalizations all help to preserve social relationships among the group. Grooming is not only a sanitary exercise, but it also serves to strengthen social relationships and form alliances.

Capuchin monkeys communicate via a sophisticated set of vocalizations, facial expressions, and body postures. They use various sounds to communicate about food sources, predators, and social interactions. For example, certain cries may indicate the presence of predators, whilst others herald the discovery of food. Facial expressions, such as bare teeth or raised brows, convey emotions and intentions, assisting in the coordination of group activities and conflict resolution.

Capuchin monkeys are noted for their lively demeanor. Juveniles participate in play fighting, chasing, and swinging from branches to develop their physical capabilities and social bonds. Play is an important part of their development, promoting cognitive growth and social learning. Adult monkeys also engage in fun exchanges that establish social relationships and minimize tensions within the group.

- Cognitive Ability and Tool Use

One of the most amazing characteristics of Capuchin monkeys is their intellect. They are well-known for their sophisticated cognitive talents, such as problem solving, tool use, and observational learning. Capuchin monkeys in the wild have been spotted utilizing tools to gather food, such as stones to crack nuts or sticks to retrieve insects from tree bark. This tool demonstrates their capacity to recognize cause-and-effect linkages and apply previously taught approaches to new situations.

According to studies, Capuchin monkeys have a great memory and can remember the location of food sources while navigating difficult situations. They can learn from one other, with younger monkeys studying and mimicking the actions of older, more experienced individuals. This social learning is an important part of their cognitive development, allowing them to learn new skills and adjust to changing circumstances.

Capuchin monkeys in captivity have been trained to execute a variety of tasks and respond to directions, demonstrating their intelligence and flexibility. However, their cognitive talents present a difficulty for pet owners, since these monkeys require continual mental stimulation and enrichment to avoid boredom and behavioral problems.

- Media Influence and Cultural Perception

The representation of Capuchin monkeys in culture and entertainment has had a considerable impact on their attractiveness as pets. These monkeys are frequently portrayed in films, television shows, and ads as adorable, clever, and entertaining companions. Famous examples include the character "Marcel" from the television series "Friends" and the mischievous monkey from the "Pirates of the Caribbean" series. These depictions promote a romanticized image of Capuchin monkeys, driving up demand among exotic pet enthusiasts.

However, the reality of owning a Capuchin monkey as a pet is significantly more challenging than media portrayals suggest. The difficulties of addressing their physical, social, and psychological demands are frequently underestimated, leading to excessive expectations among prospective buyers. The impact of media influence on the perception of Capuchin monkeys as pets must be rigorously examined, as well as the ethical issues of advocating their ownership.

- Historical Context

Capuchin monkeys have been kept as pets for centuries, first by indigenous peoples and then by European explorers. Capuchin monkeys were frequently featured in circuses, sideshows, and touring exhibitions during the nineteenth and early twentieth century, performing tricks and entertaining audiences. This historical setting has influenced the present impression of Capuchin monkeys as fascinating and engaging animals, which contributes to their popularity as pets.

In addition to their entertainment value, Capuchin monkeys have been utilized in research and as assistance animals for people with disabilities. Their intelligence and trainability make them suited for a variety of duties, including everyday assistance and companionship. However, the employment of Capuchin monkeys in research and service jobs raises ethical considerations regarding their well-being and the suitability of wild animals for human use.

- Ethical and Welfare Considerations

The decision to keep a Capuchin monkey as a pet raises serious ethical and welfare concerns. Capuchin monkeys, unlike domesticated animals like dogs and cats, are wild animals with complicated demands that are difficult to supply in a domestic environment. They need large enclosures, a diversified diet, social connection, and mental stimulation to survive. Failure to meet these basic needs might result in bodily and psychological anguish.

One of the most pressing ethical considerations is the effect on the monkeys' welfare. Capuchin monkeys in captivity frequently miss out on social and environmental enrichment that they would receive in the wild. This deprivation can result in behavioral issues such as hostility, self-mutilation, and stereotypic behaviors (repetitive, meaningless actions). Furthermore, the method of collecting and transporting wild Capuchin monkeys for the pet trade is frequently cruel, resulting in high mortality rates and suffering.

Another ethical consideration is the effect on wildlife populations. The demand for Capuchin monkeys as pets can fuel illegal trade and poaching, endangering natural populations. Capturing wild monkeys upsets their social groups, which can have a ripple impact on the ecosystem. Conservation activities are critical for protecting these species and their habitats, ensuring their long-term survival in the wild.

- Legal considerations

The legality of keeping capuchin monkeys as pets varies greatly depending on the jurisdiction. To protect both the animals and the public, certain governments and states rigorously control or prohibit the ownership of Capuchin monkeys. Prospective owners must traverse a complicated web of laws and regulations that may necessitate permits, inspections, and adherence to certain standards of care.

Where Capuchin monkey ownership is permitted, regulatory structures are in place to safeguard the animals' welfare and prevent unlawful trading. These rules may include enclosure size, feeding, veterinary care, and socialization. Compliance with these requirements is required to create a safe and healthy environment for Capuchin monkeys while avoiding legal ramifications.

- Long-Term Commitment and Responsibility

Owning a Capuchin monkey is a long-term commitment that takes considerable thought and planning. These monkeys can live up to 40 years in captivity, so prospective owners should be prepared for decades of responsibility. The financial requirements of providing proper care, which include food, shelter, veterinary care, and enrichment, can be significant. Capuchin monkeys also require a large amount of time and care because they are extremely social animals who thrive on interaction and mental stimulation.

Prospective owners must also evaluate the implications for their lifestyle and living situation. Capuchin monkeys can be demanding and difficult pets, with ongoing supervision and management. Their intelligence and curiosity might lead to negative actions if they are not sufficiently stimulated and enriched. Furthermore, Capuchin monkeys may not be suited for houses with small children or other pets since their behavior is unpredictable and potentially aggressive.

Before selecting to keep a Capuchin monkey as a pet, you should conduct extensive research and understand the obligations and problems involved. Veterinarians, primatologists, and experienced monkey owners can all contribute helpful insights and advice. Finally, the decision should be made with the monkey's welfare as the primary consideration, ensuring that their requirements are satisfied in a humane and responsible manner.

Chapter 1

Pros and Cons of Having a Capuchin Monkey

Owning a Capuchin monkey can be a unique and gratifying experience, but it also has considerable problems and obligations. Understanding the benefits and drawbacks is critical for anyone thinking about introducing one of these clever monkeys into their house.

Benefits of Having Capuchin Monkeys as Pets

- Intelligence and Trainability

Capuchin monkeys are known for their intelligence. They have high cognitive abilities that enable them to solve problems, use tools, and learn by observation and imitation. This intelligence makes them extremely trainable, and they can be taught a wide range of duties and tricks. For example, Capuchin monkeys have been trained to help people with disabilities by fetching belongings, opening doors, and turning lights on and off. Their ability to learn and adapt makes them interesting and entertaining companions.

- Emotional bonding and companionship

Capuchin monkeys are gregarious animals who build close ties with their human caregivers. When nurtured in a supportive setting, they can develop into affectionate and interactive pets. A Capuchin monkey and its owner can form a strong emotional bond, offering company and lessening feelings of loneliness. This link might be especially advantageous for people who want a close and involved relationship with their pets.

- Unusual and entertaining behavior

Capuchin monkeys perform a variety of actions that are both interesting and captivating to see. Their playful behavior, curiosity, and agility make them entertaining to watch. They are noted for their inquisitive temperament and may participate in complicated play activities including as investigating their surroundings, manipulating items, and communicating with other pets. This habit can give limitless fun and enrichment to its owners.

- Educational Opportunities

Having a Capuchin monkey can provide excellent educational possibilities. Observing and caring for clever monkeys can help you better understand animal behavior, cognition, and social dynamics. It can help instill a better respect for wildlife and conservation activities. A Capuchin monkey may be a fascinating and educational companion for youngsters, teaching them about responsibility, empathy, and the necessity of animal care.

- Potential for service and therapy roles

Capuchin monkeys have been successfully taught to work as service animals and in therapeutic settings. Their dexterity and intellect enable them to do jobs that benefit people with physical impairments. Furthermore, their presence can be therapeutic, offering comfort and company to those in hospitals, nursing homes, and other care facilities. The usage of Capuchin monkeys in these jobs demonstrates their ability to improve the quality of life for persons who require help and emotional support.

Challenges and Drawbacks

- Complex Care Requirements

Capuchin monkeys have complicated and unique care requirements that can be difficult to manage in a household setting. They require a well-balanced diet rich in fresh fruits and vegetables, proteins, and specialized monkey chow. Proper diet is vital for avoiding health problems including malnutrition and obesity. In addition to a healthy food, Capuchin monkeys require a large and enriching environment that provides for physical exercise and mental stimulation. Adequate habitat, such as big and safe enclosures with climbing platforms and interactive toys, is critical to their well-being.

- Behavioral Challenges

Capuchin monkeys, despite their intelligence and trainability, can engage in demanding behaviors. They are extremely active and curious animals who can become destructive if not properly stimulated. Boredom and a lack of mental stimulation can rise to actions like aggression, biting, and destructive chewing. Managing these behaviors necessitates continual supervision, teaching, and the provision of stimulating activities to keep them engaged.

- Social and Psychological Needs

Capuchin monkeys are gregarious creatures who flourish in the company of their own species. In the wild, they form intricate social groupings and participate in grooming, play, and social interactions. When maintained as pets, they may experience loneliness and social deprivation if they do not have regular connection with other monkeys or their human caregivers. Meeting their social and psychological needs takes a large amount of time and effort, which includes regular socialization, play, and enrichment activities.

- Health and Veterinary Care

Capuchin monkeys require specialist veterinary treatment from experts in primate medicine. Finding a skilled veterinarian can be difficult, and medical treatment for exotic pets can be expensive. Regular health checks, immunizations, and preventive care are required to protect the safety of Capuchin monkeys. They are also prone to a variety of health problems, such as lung infections, gastrointestinal disorders, and dental ailments, which necessitate immediate and adequate treatment.

- Legal and Regulatory Challenges

The legality of possessing Capuchin monkeys varies by region, and potential owners must traverse a complicated web of laws and restrictions. Keeping Capuchin monkeys as pets is strictly regulated or forbidden in many locations to protect both the animals and the general population. Obtaining the proper permits and meeting regulatory criteria can be a time-consuming and difficult task. Furthermore, changes in regulation can affect the capacity to own and care for Capuchin monkeys, causing ambiguity and potential legal concerns for owners.

- Long-term commitment

Capuchin monkeys have a long lifespan, frequently reaching 40 years in captivity. This longevity necessitates a long-term investment by their owners, both in terms of time and cash. Prospective owners must be prepared to assume decades of duty, including daily care, social engagement, and enrichment. The financial costs of owning a Capuchin monkey can be high, including food, housing, veterinary care, and enrichment goods.

- Ethical considerations

The ethical concerns of keeping Capuchin monkeys as pets are an important consideration. Capuchin monkeys, as wild creatures with complex needs, may suffer in captivity if their living conditions do not appropriately mirror their natural habitat. Capturing and transporting wild monkeys for the pet trade is typically brutal, with high fatality rates. Furthermore, the desire for Capuchin monkeys as pets can lead to illegal trading and poaching, endangering wild populations and altering ecosystems.

- Impact on the Human Lifestyle

Owning a Capuchin monkey can have a profound impact on the lives of its human caregivers. These primates demand regular attention and monitoring, making long-term separation difficult.

Their care needs can make it difficult for them to travel, participate in social activities, and go about their everyday lives. Furthermore, the presence of a Capuchin monkey in the home may cause problems for families with young children or other pets, as their behavior can be unpredictable and sometimes hostile.

Owning a Capuchin monkey as a pet presents a unique set of advantages and disadvantages. Their intelligence, emotional bonding, and entertaining behavior make them intriguing and appealing companions. However, prospective owners have substantial obstacles in meeting their care requirements, managing behavioral issues, and addressing their social and psychological needs. Legal, ethical, and long-term commitment considerations emphasize the obligations associated with owning a Capuchin monkey.

Before making a decision, prospective owners should carefully assess the advantages and disadvantages, extensively understand the requirements and obligations, and consider the monkey's well-being. Consulting with specialists and experienced monkey owners can provide useful information and advice. Finally, the decision to keep a Capuchin monkey as a pet should prioritize the animal's well-being, ensuring that its requirements are satisfied in a humane and responsible manner.

Chapter 2

Legal considerations

Keeping a Capuchin monkey as a pet requires navigating a complicated environment of laws and restrictions that differ greatly depending on the country, state, or municipality. These legislative frameworks are intended to ensure animal welfare, protect public safety, and prohibit the unlawful trafficking of alien species. Understanding and adhering to these laws is critical for potential Capuchin monkey owners to prevent legal ramifications and assure ethical care of their pets.

International laws

The Convention on International Trade in Endangered Wild Fauna and Flora (CITES)

CITES is an international agreement among states to ensure that international trade in wild animals and plants does not endanger their survival. Capuchin monkeys, like many other exotic animals, are protected by CITES, which oversees their trade through a system of licenses and limits. Capuchin monkeys may be included in several CITES appendices based on the species and level of protection necessary. For example, species included in Appendix I are deemed at risk of extinction and are subject to the most stringent rules, including a ban on commercial trade. Prospective owners must be informed of the restrictions and secure the relevant permits before importing or exporting Capuchin monkeys.

World Animal Protection and Welfare Acts

Several worldwide organizations and agreements are dedicated to animal welfare and ethical treatment of animals. These include the World Animal Protection Act and individual animal welfare laws enacted by several countries. These frameworks offer principles for ethical animal treatment, as well as criteria for their care and housing. Prospective Capuchin monkey owners should educate themselves with these recommendations to guarantee that their pets have a safe and ethical environment.

National and State Laws

- The United States

In the United States, the legality of possessing Capuchin monkeys as pets varies greatly by state. Some states expressly prohibit owning primates, while others have strict laws and permit requirements.

- Federal regulations

At the federal level, the United States. The regulation of exotic species, such as Capuchin monkeys, is overseen by the USDA and the Fish and Wildlife Service (FWS). The USDA's Animal Welfare Act (AWA) establishes guidelines for the care and treatment of animals used in research, exhibition, and commerce, including primates maintained as pets. The FWS oversees the import and export of wildlife under the Endangered Species Act (ESA) and the Lacey Act, which restricts the trading of illegally obtained animals.

- State Regulations

The ownership of Capuchin monkeys is governed by different legislation in each state. Private possession of primates, such as Capuchin monkeys, is strictly prohibited in California and New York. In contrast, jurisdictions like as Florida and Texas allow ownership with certain permits and rules. These restrictions frequently include provisions for housing, veterinary care, and public safety precautions. To legally acquire a Capuchin monkey, prospective owners must first check their state's unique legislation and secure the relevant permits.

- The European Union

In the European Union, Capuchin monkey ownership is governed by both EU-wide rules and specific member state laws. The EU's Wildlife Trade Regulations enforce CITES within the EU by regulating the import, export, and movement of listed species, including Capuchin monkeys. Furthermore, the EU's Animal Welfare Directive establishes guidelines for the treatment and care of animals, including exotic pets. Member states may have extra rules that prospective owners must follow.

- Other Countries

Other countries have varying laws regarding the ownership of Capuchin monkeys. Some countries, such as Australia, have strong exotic pet ownership bans in place to safeguard native species and ecosystems. Others, such as Japan, allow ownership with certain permits and laws. Prospective pet owners must research and grasp the rules and regulations in their respective countries or regions to ensure compliance and ethical treatment of their pets.

Local and Municipal Regulations

In addition to national and state rules, local communities may have their own regulations governing Capuchin monkey ownership. These rules may include zoning legislation, housing requirements, and public safety measures. Some cities, for example, may have rules prohibiting the harboring of exotic animals inside city limits or requiring special permissions and inspections. Prospective owners must consult with their local government to understand and follow any additional regulations.

Permit and Licensing

Obtaining the proper permits and licenses for owning a Capuchin monkey is an important step toward guaranteeing legal compliance and ethical treatment of the animal. The method and requirements for acquiring licenses vary by jurisdiction, but generally comprise the following steps:

- Application Process

The first step in obtaining a permit to possess a Capuchin monkey is to file an application with the appropriate authorities. This application often requests comprehensive information about the potential owner, such as their experience with unusual animals, the monkey's anticipated housing and care arrangements, and the reason for ownership (e.g., personal pet, educational exhibit, service animal). The application procedure may also include background checks and references to ensure that the prospective owner is qualified and capable of providing adequate care.

- Inspection and Approval

After the application is submitted, authorities may check the prospective owner's facilities to confirm that they fulfill the necessary criteria for housing and care. This inspection usually involves an assessment of the enclosure's size and design, environmental enrichment, diet and nutrition, and veterinarian care plans. If the facilities meet the necessary standards, the permit may be approved. In some circumstances, authorities may issue particular suggestions or conditions that must be followed before final clearance is granted.

- Permit Fees and Renewal

Obtaining a permission to keep a Capuchin monkey frequently requires paying application and renewal fees. These fees vary according to the jurisdiction and type of permit necessary. Furthermore, permits are usually only valid for a short time (for example, one year) and must be renewed on a regular basis. Renewals may include re-inspections and updated documents to verify continuous regulatory compliance.

- Record-keeping and Reporting

In general, permit holders must keep complete records of their Capuchin monkeys' care and treatment. This includes information about veterinary appointments, health status, food, and any incidents or behavioral difficulties. Authorities may require frequent reports or inspections to verify regulatory compliance. Failure to keep accurate records and comply with reporting requirements may result in fines, revocation of the permit, or confiscation of the animal.

- Transport and Movement

Moving a Capuchin monkey across state or national borders frequently necessitates additional permissions and compliance with certain rules. This includes securing import and export permissions, maintaining proper quarantine processes, and following transportation requirements to protect the animal's welfare. Prospective owners of Capuchin monkeys must be aware of these restrictions and arrange accordingly if they desire to transport them.

- Public Safety and Liability Insurance

Some countries require permit holders to demonstrate that they have suitable safeguards in place to ensure public safety. This could include secure enclosures, safety guidelines for handling the monkey, and liability insurance to cover any injuries or damage caused by the animal. Ensuring public safety is a vital component of responsible ownership and legal compliance.

Ethical and Welfare Considerations

While legal compliance is critical, ethical and welfare considerations are just as crucial when owning a Capuchin monkey. These issues extend beyond completing legal standards to assuring the animal's welfare and compassionate treatment.

- Offering Adequate Housing and Enrichment

Capuchin monkeys require large, enriched surroundings that allow for physical activity, mental stimulation, and social contact. This includes creating big enclosures with climbing structures, engaging toys, and possibilities for exploration. To promote the monkey's well-being, owners must ensure that its surroundings closely resembles that of its natural habitat.

- Ensure proper nutrition and health care.

Capuchin monkeys require a well-balanced and varied diet to maintain their health. This contains fresh fruits, vegetables, meats, and specialty primate food. Regular veterinarian care from doctors who specialize in primate medicine is also essential. To preserve the monkey's long-term health, owners must take a proactive approach to health issues and provide preventive care.

- Addressing Social and Psychological Needs

Capuchin monkeys are extremely social creatures who thrive on interaction and company. Owners must provide regular socialization and enrichment activities to avoid loneliness and behavioral difficulties. This includes spending quality time with the monkey, allowing for play and social interaction, and contemplating the potential advantages of having numerous monkeys to suit their social needs.

- Ethical Considerations for Captivity

The ethical issues of keeping Capuchin monkeys captive are substantial. As wild creatures, they may face confinement and deprivation if their requirements are not fulfilled correctly. Prospective owners must assess if they can create a setting that promotes monkey welfare while adhering to ethical animal-treatment norms. This includes assessing the potential influence on the monkey's physical and psychological health and ensuring that the decision to purchase a Capuchin monkey is driven by a genuine concern for the animal's well-being.

- Contributing to Conservation and Education.

Responsible ownership of Capuchin monkeys include contributing to conservation efforts and raising awareness of the species. Owners can support conservation efforts that protect wild populations and their habitats. Additionally, educating others on the intricacies and responsibilities of keeping Capuchin monkeys can help lower the desire for exotic pets while also promoting ethical animal treatment.

Keeping a Capuchin monkey as a pet entails navigating a complicated and varied landscape of legal concerns, ethical duties, and practical problems. Understanding and adhering to the applicable rules and regulations is critical to ensuring the legal and ethical treatment of these clever and sensitive animals. This includes getting the relevant permits, complying with housing and care requirements, and assuring public safety.

Beyond legal compliance, potential owners must examine the ethical implications of keeping Capuchin monkeys in captivity and prioritise their welfare. Adequate housing, nourishment, social interaction, and veterinary care are critical for maintaining the monkey's health and pleasure. Supporting conservation initiatives and teaching others about the responsibilities of exotic pet ownership can also help to protect and treat Capuchin monkeys and other species ethically.

Finally, the decision to purchase a Capuchin monkey should be taken after thorough evaluation of the animal's requirements and welfare, with a focus on providing a compassionate and responsible environment. Prospective owners can make informed and responsible decisions that benefit both the monkeys and the larger community by first learning and resolving the legal and ethical elements of ownership.

Chapter 3

Care Needs for Capuchin Monkeys

Having a Capuchin monkey involves a strong commitment to providing comprehensive care that addresses their physical, psychological, and social requirements. These educated and energetic primates have special needs in terms of housing, diet, and healthcare. Ensuring that these needs are satisfied is critical to their health and quality of life.

Housing and Habitat

Enclosure Size and Design

Capuchin monkeys are extremely active and require large enclosures that allow them plenty of movement and exercise. The enclosure should be large enough to allow both vertical and horizontal space for the monkey to climb, jump, and explore. A single Capuchin monkey should be kept in an enclosure that is at least 10 feet by 10 feet by 10 feet, but larger enclosures are always preferred. The enclosure should be made to closely resemble their natural habitat, with multiple levels, climbing structures, and perches.

- Materials & Construction

The enclosure should be made with durable materials that can resist the monkey's strength and activity. Strong metal mesh or bars are ideal for preventing escapes and maintaining safety. To avoid injuries, the flooring should be easy to clean and slip-resistant. If used outside, enclosures should be waterproof to protect against excessive temperatures and adverse weather conditions.

- Environmental Enrichment

Capuchin monkeys are bright and curious, thus they require a dynamic environment to avoid boredom and behavioral problems. The cage should feature enrichment devices like ropes, swings, ladders, and puzzle feeders. Regularly rotating and introducing new enrichment items helps keep the monkey interested and mentally active. Natural components such as branches, leaves, and rocks can also be used to create a more realistic atmosphere.

- Safety & Security

Safety is crucial while planning and maintaining the enclosure. It should be escape-proof, with sturdy locks and latches. Regular inspections are required to ensure there are no weak areas or damage that could allow escapes. Furthermore, the enclosure must be clear of sharp things and hazardous materials that could endanger the monkey.

Social Environment

Capuchin monkeys are highly social animals who thrive on interaction with others. To meet their social needs, they should ideally be able to interact with other Capuchin monkeys. However, if having numerous monkeys is not an option, owners must devote significant time to socializing with their pet to avoid loneliness and sadness.

- Human Interaction

A Capuchin monkey's psychological well-being depends on regular interactions with human caretakers. This engagement should involve play, grooming, and training sessions. Consistent socializing fosters a deep link between the monkey and its caregiver, offering emotional support and mental stimulation.

- Interaction With Other Animals

If maintaining numerous Capuchin monkeys is not an option, introducing the monkey to other suitable pets, such as dogs or birds, can give additional social interaction. However, these encounters must be properly monitored to guarantee safety and avoid hostility or injury.

Hygiene and cleanliness

Maintaining a clean and sanitary environment is critical to the health of Capuchin monkeys. The enclosure should be cleaned on a regular basis to remove trash, uneaten food, and other dirt. Bedding materials should be replaced on a regular basis, and food and drink containers should be cleaned regularly to prevent bacterial growth and contamination.

- Cleaning Protocols

To preserve hygiene, create a regular cleaning program. This involves daily spot cleaning of the cage, weekly full cleaning of all surfaces and enrichment items, and monthly disinfection to avoid illness transmission. To protect the monkey's safety, utilize nontoxic cleaning chemicals.

- Health Monitoring

Regular monitoring of the monkey's health is necessary. Any changes in behavior, appetite, or physical condition should be observed and addressed immediately. Maintaining detailed health records can assist in tracking the monkey's well-being and detecting potential health issues early on.

Diet & Nutrition

Capuchin monkeys require a well-balanced diet similar to what they would eat in the wild. Their diet should consist of a mix of fresh fruits, vegetables, proteins, and specialized primate food. A good diet is vital for avoiding nutritional deficits and health problems.

- Fruit and Vegetable

A large amount of a Capuchin monkey's diet should include fresh fruits and vegetables. Common fruits include apples, bananas, grapes, and berries, while veggies include carrots, sweet potatoes, leafy greens, and bell peppers. These provide important vitamins, minerals, and fibre. To promote a balanced nutrient intake, serve a variety of fruits and vegetables.

- Proteins

Proteins are essential for the development and maintenance of bodily tissues. Capuchin monkeys can get protein from foods like eggs, roasted chicken, insects, and nuts. Animal proteins should be well cooked to avoid bacterial infections, and nuts should be consumed in moderation due to their high fat content.

- Specialized Primate Chow

Specialized primate chow is designed to fulfill monkeys' nutritional needs and should be included in their diets. This chow supplies important nutrients that may be lacking in a diet consisting primarily of fruits and vegetables. It is critical to use high-quality primate food and follow the manufacturer's feeding recommendations.

Feeding practices

- Meal frequency

Capuchin monkeys should be fed several short meals each day rather than one or two large meals. This matches their natural food patterns, hence preventing overeating and obesity. A normal feeding plan may include three to four meals per day, with a variety of fruits, vegetables, proteins, and primate chow.

- Portion Control

Proper portion control is vital for avoiding obesity and maintaining a healthy diet. Owners should monitor the monkey's weight and modify portions accordingly. Treats should be offered sparingly and not make up a large component of the diet.

- Hydration

Fresh, clean water should always be available. Water containers should be checked and replaced on a daily basis, and regular cleaning is required to prevent contamination. Some Capuchin monkeys may prefer to drink from water bottles, but others may favor bowls. Providing both alternatives can help guarantee proper hydration.

Nutritional Supplements

In some situations, nutritional supplements may be required to maintain a balanced diet. These may include vitamin and mineral supplements, probiotics, and omega-3 fatty acids. However, supplements should only be administered under the supervision of a veterinarian to avoid over-supplementation and associated health risks.

- Common Supplements

Calcium and vitamin D are popular supplements for Capuchin monkeys, as are vitamin C and omega-3 fatty acids for skin and coat health. Probiotics can also help preserve intestinal health.

- Consult a veterinarian

It is critical to consult a veterinarian before introducing any supplements into the monkey's diet. A veterinarian can evaluate the monkey's nutritional requirements and provide appropriate vitamins and dosages.

Health and Veterinary Care

Regular Health Checkups

Regular veterinarian examinations are necessary to monitor the health of Capuchin monkeys and prevent future health problems. These check-ups should be performed by a veterinarian who is familiar with primate care and should involve a comprehensive physical examination, blood testing, and dental exams.

- Checkup Frequency

Capuchin monkeys should have annual health checks. Younger monkeys, the elderly, or those with pre-existing health concerns may require more regular visits. Regular check-ups aid in the early detection of health disorders and ensure appropriate treatment.

- Vaccinations

Capuchin monkeys receive vaccinations as part of their preventive health care. Rabies, tetanus, and other vaccines suggested by the veterinarian are among the most common. To ensure the monkey's immunity to infections, vaccination schedules should be strictly adhered to.

Common Health Issues:

Capuchin monkeys are prone to a variety of health problems that require immediate attention and treatment. Knowing about these frequent health conditions and their symptoms can help owners take preventative actions to maintain their monkey's well-being.

- Respiratory infections

Capuchin monkeys frequently develop respiratory infections, which can be caused by bacteria, viruses, or fungi. Symptoms include coughing, sneezing, nasal drainage, and difficulty breathing. Diagnosing and treating respiratory illnesses requires prompt veterinarian attention.

- Gastrointestinal Problems

Dietary disorders, viruses, and parasites can all cause gastrointestinal problems like diarrhea, constipation, and bloating. Symptoms may include changes in appetite, vomiting, and stool consistency. A healthy diet, good hygiene, and regular veterinarian treatment can help prevent and manage gastrointestinal disorders.

- Dental Issues

Capuchin monkeys frequently suffer from dental problems such as tooth decay, gum disease, and abscess. Regular dental check-ups and adequate dental hygiene, such as brushing and using appropriate chew toys, can assist to maintain dental health. Drooling, difficulty eating, and face swelling are all symptoms of a tooth problem.

- Skin and Coat Problems

Capuchin monkeys may suffer from skin and coat issues such as dry skin, dermatitis, and parasite infestations. Regular grooming, a balanced diet, and timely treatment of skin problems are all necessary for keeping healthy skin and coat. Itching, hair loss, and visible skin lesions are some of the symptoms.

Emergency Care

Owners of Capuchin monkeys should have an emergency care plan in place. This involves knowing the location of the nearest emergency veterinary clinic that specializes in primate care and keeping an emergency kit on hand.

- Emergency Kit

An emergency pack should include antiseptic wipes, bandages, tweezers, a digital thermometer, and any necessary drugs. Owners should also keep a transport carrier on hand for quick journeys to the veterinarian in the event of an emergency.

- Emergency Contact Information

It is critical to have the primary veterinarian's contact information and the location of the nearest emergency veterinary clinic on hand. Owners should also carry a list of emergency procedures and first aid supplies on hand to provide rapid care while traveling to the veterinarian.

Preventive Health Measures

Implementing preventative health practices can reduce the likelihood of health problems and improve the overall well-being of Capuchin monkeys.

- Hygiene and Sanitation

Keeping a clean and sanitary atmosphere is essential for avoiding infections and diseases. This involves routine cleaning and disinfection of the enclosure, food and water containers, and enrichment materials. Proper waste management and insect control are also essential for preventing disease transmission.

- Diet & Nutrition

A balanced and nutritious meal is critical for keeping the monkey healthy and preventing nutritional deficits and other health problems. Monitoring the monkey's weight and modifying the diet as necessary can help prevent obesity and other diet-related issues.

- Mental and Physical Stimulation

Regular mental and physical stimulation through environmental enrichment, social interaction, and training exercises is critical to the monkey's psychological well-being. Boredom and a lack of excitement can cause behavioral disorders and stress-related health concerns.

- Stress Management

Capuchin monkeys' health depends heavily on reducing stress. This includes maintaining a stable and predictable environment, minimizing abrupt changes, and promoting regular social engagement and enrichment. Recognizing and resolving indicators of stress, such as behavioral or appetite changes, is critical for avoiding stress-related health problems.

Caring for a Capuchin monkey is a huge responsibility that necessitates a strong dedication to meeting their complicated requirements. Their well-being depends on adequate housing, a balanced nutrition, and frequent health treatment. Understanding and meeting their physical, psychological, and social requirements can help these intelligent and sensitive creatures live happy and healthy lives. By focusing on their care and well-being, owners can form a strong and gratifying attachment with their Capuchin monkey, improving their overall quality of life.

Chapter 4

Behavior and Training

Capuchin monkeys are noted for their intelligence, curiosity, and intricate social behavior. Understanding these behaviors and meeting their socialization needs is critical for giving appropriate care and maintaining a healthy and harmonious relationship between monkey and owner. Training, when done effectively, can improve communication, enrich the monkey's surroundings, and avoid or alleviate behavioral difficulties.

Typical behaviors

Capuchin monkeys have a diverse set of behaviors that represent their social nature, intellect, and adaptability. Recognizing and comprehending these behaviors is critical for delivering proper care and addressing any problems.

Social behaviors

- Grooming

Grooming is a typical social action among Capuchin monkeys, and it serves several functions, including hygiene, bonding, and social hierarchy reinforcement. Grooming involves one monkey scrubbing another's fur to eliminate filth, parasites, and dead skin. It also strengthens social relationships and fosters trust among individuals. Owners may witness their Capuchin monkey grooming themselves or attempting to groom their caregivers or other pets.

- Play

Play is an important part of Capuchin monkeys' social lives and growth. Young monkeys, in particular, engage in active play that includes chasing, wrestling, and mimic fighting. Play promotes physical coordination, social skills, and cognitive capacities. Providing adequate opportunities for play is critical for the monkey's overall well-being and can help minimize boredom and anxiety.

- Social Hierarchy

Capuchin monkeys form intricate social groupings with established hierarchies. Dominance hierarchies govern access to resources, mating opportunities, and social interactions.

Understanding the social dynamics and hierarchy of Capuchin monkeys is critical for controlling their behavior and preventing disputes. Owners of many monkeys should be aware of these hierarchies and manage interactions to maintain a happy group dynamic.

- Communication

Capuchin monkeys communicate with one another through a variety of vocalizations, facial expressions, and gestures. Common vocalizations include chirps, whistles, screams, and barks, which each serve a distinct purpose, such as sounding an alarm, drawing attention, or expressing satisfaction. Understanding these communication cues can aid owners in interpreting their monkey's needs and feelings.

Cognitive behaviors

- Problem-Solving

Capuchin monkeys are extremely bright and skilled problem solvers. They can manipulate objects, use tools, and devise novel solutions to problems. Enrichment activities that foster problem-solving, such as puzzle feeders or interactive toys, might help them retain their cognitive talents and avoid boredom.

- Memory & Learning

Capuchin monkeys have excellent memories and can learn difficult tasks with observation and repetition. They are able to learn by imitation and retain learnt habits for extended periods. Positive reinforcement training methods that use their memory and learning capacities can be extremely effective.

- Curiosity and Exploration

Capuchin monkeys are naturally interested and like exploring their surroundings. To better grasp their surroundings, they will study new objects, manipulate items, and try out various actions. Owners should create a dynamic and enriching environment that promotes inquiry and fulfills curiosity.

Emotional behaviors

- Affection and Bonding

Capuchin monkeys build close ties with both their caregivers and other monkeys. They may express affection by grooming, cuddling, or seeking physical contact. Building a deep bond with a Capuchin monkey requires continuous and positive interactions, such as play, grooming, and gentle handling.

- Stress & Anxiety

Capuchin monkeys can suffer stress and anxiety, which can lead to behavioral changes such as increased aggression, self-injury, or withdrawal. Identifying and managing stressors, such as changes in routine, a lack of social connection, or inadequate enrichment, is critical to their well-being. Creating a secure and predictable environment, as well as regular social engagement and enrichment, can help reduce stress and anxiety.

- Aggression

Capuchin monkeys can become aggressive, particularly when there is rivalry for resources, social hierarchy issues, or perceived threats. Understanding aggressiveness triggers and using appropriate management methods, such as providing separate feeding places and monitoring interactions, can assist to prevent confrontations and maintain a safe and harmonious environment.

Socialization Needs

Capuchin monkeys have complex social demands that must be met in order to maintain their psychological well-being. Socialization entails socializing with other monkeys, people, and even other pets, and is critical to their mental and emotional wellbeing.

Interaction with Other Monkeys

- Group Living

Capuchin monkeys live in social groups in the wild, and keeping them in captivity in couples or groups can help them meet their social interaction needs. Group life allows for social bonding, play, grooming, and hierarchy formation. Owners should make sure the monkeys have ample space to interact and form a social structure.

- Introducing New Monkeys

Introducing a new monkey into an established group necessitates careful planning and gradual integration. Initial introductions should take place in a neutral setting, with the monkeys regularly observed for symptoms of hostility or discomfort. Gradual increases in the duration and frequency of contacts can help monkeys adjust to each other and form healthy connections.

Interaction With Humans

- Bonding and Trust-building

Developing a deep bond with a Capuchin monkey requires continuous and good encounters. Caregivers should spend time with the monkey every day, engaging in activities such as play, grooming, and training. Positive reinforcement, gentle handling, and patience are essential for creating trust and a strong bond.

- Social Interaction

Regular social connection with human caregivers is critical to the monkey's psychological well-being. This relationship should involve verbal communication, physical contact, and enrichment activities. Owners should pay attention to the monkey's social signs and tailor their interactions to suit the monkey's requirements and preferences.

Interaction With Other Pets

- Compatibility

Capuchin monkeys can engage with other pets, such as dogs, cats, and birds, as long as the relationships are carefully monitored and handled. The compatibility of the monkey and the other pets is determined by their individual personalities. Initial introductions should be made gradually, and interactions should be properly monitored to guarantee safety and avoid aggressiveness or stress.

- Supervised Interactions:

Supervised interactions between the monkey and other pets are essential for preventing confrontations and ensuring safety. If owners notice any signs of hostility or tension, they should act and, if necessary, separate the monkey and other pets.

Training Tips

Training Capuchin monkeys is critical for their cerebral stimulation, socializing, and behavior control. Positive reinforcement approaches are especially useful for educating these sophisticated monkeys.

Positive Reinforcement

- Rewards

Positive reinforcement entails rewarding desired behaviors with treats, praise, or other types of positive stimuli. To strengthen the association, rewards should be delivered promptly after doing the desired behavior. Small bits of fruit, nuts, or other favored foods are commonly given as rewards.

- Consistency

Consistency is essential in educating Capuchin monkeys. Owners should employ consistent cues, orders, and rewards to encourage desirable behaviours. To keep the monkey engaged and attentive, training sessions should be regular and short, lasting no more than 10-15 minutes.

- Patience & Persistence

Patience and persistence are required while training capuchin monkeys. Progress may be slow, and setbacks are frequent.

Owners should exercise patience and avoid punishment or negative reinforcement, which can escalate to fear and hostility.

Basic commands and behaviors.

- Come when called

Teaching a capuchin monkey to come when called is a basic instruction that improves safety and control. Begin by giving the monkey a specific verbal cue or whistle and rewarding it when it approaches. Gradually increase the command's distance and complexity.

- Sit

Teaching the "sit" command can assist manage the monkey's behavior and lay the groundwork for more complex training. Use a verbal cue and a hand signal to reward the monkey when it sits. Consistent repetition and reinforcement can strengthen the behavior.

- Stay

The "stay" command is useful for directing the monkey's actions and guaranteeing its safety. Use a verbal cue and a hand signal to reward the monkey for remaining in place. Gradually extend the time and distance of the command.

Advanced Training

- Target Training

Target training teaches the monkey to contact a specific object, such as a stick or a target, with its hand or nose. This can be used to control the monkey's movements and behavior. Use a target stick and reward the monkey for touching it. Gradually raise the complexity of the duties.

- Problem-solving tasks

Problem-solving tasks can help the monkey's cognitive ability and prevent boredom. These tasks can include puzzle feeders, interactive toys, and training sessions in which the monkey must figure out how to get a reward. Use positive reinforcement to stimulate problem-solving and reward the monkey when it completes the task successfully.

- Trick Training

Capuchin monkeys can enjoy and benefit from learning tasks like waving, spinning, and retrieving objects. Teach each trick using positive reinforcement and consistent cues, progressively increasing its complexity and difficulty.

Addressing Behavior Issues

- Aggression

Capuchin monkeys can become aggressive for a variety of reasons, including fear, stress, and social hierarchy issues. Addressing aggression entails determining the root reason and applying suitable management methods. Separate feeding places, stress reduction, and positive reward can all help to promote calm behavior.

- Self-Injury

Self-injury, such as hair pulling or biting, might be indicative of stress or boredom. Addressing self-injury entails improving the environment, boosting social connection, and addressing sources of stress. Veterinary care may be required to address any underlying health concerns.

- Destructive Behavior

Boredom and a lack of excitement can lead to destructive conduct, such as chewing on furniture or damaging belongings. Providing suitable toys, enrichment activities, and monitoring can help to redirect the monkey's behavior and prevent damage. Positive reward for acceptable behaviors can also motivate the monkey to participate in more appropriate activities.

Understanding Capuchin monkey behavior and training demands is critical for providing them with a rewarding and enriching existence in captivity. By identifying their social, cognitive, and emotional characteristics, owners may foster a positive atmosphere that supports their well-being and prevents behavioral difficulties. Positive reinforcement and consistency-based training strategies can enhance the attachment between a monkey and its owner while also improving communication and understanding. Capuchin monkeys, with adequate care, socialization, and training, can thrive as clever and interesting companions in responsible and knowledgeable households.

Chapter 5

Costs and Financial Commitments for Owning a Capuchin Monkey

Owning a Capuchin monkey requires significant financial investment, including initial purchasing and setup expenditures, as well as ongoing spending for housing, feeding, veterinary care, and other essentials. Understanding these expenditures is critical for prospective owners who want to make educated decisions and create a secure and supportive environment for their primate companions.

Initial Costs

Acquisition

- Purchase Price:

The initial cost of purchasing a Capuchin monkey varies greatly based on the monkey's age, health, disposition, and whether it comes from a breeder, rescue group, or individual sale. Prices might vary from a few thousand to tens of thousands of dollars. Monkeys that are younger or trained for specific duties may fetch a greater price.

- Legal and Permit Fees

Depending on local rules, obtaining a Capuchin monkey may necessitate a permit or license. These expenses vary greatly by location and usually include application fees, inspection costs, and annual renewal fees. It is critical to conduct study and comply with all legal regulations in order to avoid penalties and ensure the monkey's legal status.

Housing and Enclosure Setup

- Enclosure Costs

Building or purchasing a suitable habitat for a Capuchin monkey requires a large upfront investment. The enclosure should be large, secure, and filled with climbing equipment, perches, and enrichment items. Enclosures can cost anywhere from a few thousand dollars to tens of thousands, depending on size, materials, and personalization.

- Environmental Enrichment

Providing a stimulating environment is critical for the monkey's health. Enrichment elements like ropes, swings, puzzle feeders, and toys should be included in the enclosure design. These objects stimulate natural habits, reduce boredom, and promote physical and mental exercise. Budgeting for first enrichment items is critical for creating an engaging environment from the start.

Veterinary Exam and Initial Care

- Health Examination

When purchasing a Capuchin monkey, it is necessary to have a thorough health assessment performed by a trained veterinarian with knowledge in primate care. This examination evaluates the monkey's overall health, identifies any existing health concerns, and sets a baseline for future care. Veterinary prices for initial examinations can range from several hundred to more than a thousand dollars, depending on the scope of the evaluation and any necessary tests.

- Vaccination and Preventive Care

Capuchin monkeys must be immunized against diseases like rabies and tetanus, among other hazards. Vaccination expenses vary depending on the exact vaccines needed and veterinary fees. Furthermore, preventive treatment such as deworming, flea and tick control, and grooming may incur additional costs during the early period of ownership.

Training and socialization

- Training Materials and Tools

Investing in training materials and techniques is essential for instilling healthy behaviors and routines in a Capuchin monkey. This could include clickers, target sticks, leashes, and other training tools. These technologies improve communication, encourage desired behaviors with positive reinforcement, and foster attachment between the monkey and its human. Budgeting for these tools ensures that training begins quickly and effectively.

- Socialization Activities

Socialization is critical for the monkey's emotional well-being and adaptability to its new surroundings. Visits to safe outside locations, introductions to other appropriate pets or animals, and supervised encounters with people are all possible socialization activities to budget for. These activities help the monkey establish trust, social skills, and minimize the stress involved with moving to a new home.

Ongoing expenses

- Housing & Maintenance

Regular cleaning, sanitization, and care of structures and enrichment items are required to maintain the monkey enclosure. Routine care keeps the monkey in a safe and sanitary environment and prevents the accumulation of excrement, bacteria, and other toxins. Budgeting for cleaning materials, replacement of worn-out equipment, and regular maintenance aids in the enclosure's integrity and functionality.

- Utilities

Depending on the enclosure's location, recurring costs may include utilities like energy for heating or cooling systems, lighting, and water supply. Providing a suitable and climate-controlled habitat is critical to the monkey's health and well-being, especially in areas with extreme temperatures or seasonal fluctuations.

Diet & Nutrition

- Food & Supplements

Capuchin monkeys require a well-balanced diet that includes fresh fruits, vegetables, meats, and specialty primate chow. Budgeting for continuous food costs ensures that the monkey has a constant and nutritious diet that matches its nutritional requirements. Furthermore, supplements such as vitamins, minerals, and probiotics may be required to maintain good health, especially if dietary deficits are discovered.

- Food Prep and Storage

Proper meal preparation and storage are required to prevent infection and assure the monkey's food safety. This could include buying food in bulk, preparing fresh meals every day, and storing perishable foods in appropriate containers or refrigeration.

Budgeting for food preparation materials and storage solutions promotes good nutrition and diet management.

Veterinary Care and Health Maintenance

- Routine check-ups

Regular veterinary examinations are essential for monitoring the monkey's health, detecting early signs of illness or damage, and implementing preventive measures. Budgeting for annual or biannual veterinarian visits ensures that health evaluations are conducted on a regular basis and that interventions are implemented as needed. Veterinary prices might vary depending on the scope of the examination, diagnostic tests, and recommended treatments.

- Emergency Veterinary Care

Unexpected health situations may arise, necessitating rapid veterinary attention. Budgeting for emergency veterinary care ensures that you are financially prepared for any necessary medical treatments, diagnostic tests, prescriptions, or hospitalization. Having access to emergency veterinary services that specialize in primate care is critical for prompt and successful treatment.

Enrichment and Behavioral Needs

- Enrichment Items

Continuously offering fresh and engaging enrichment items is critical for reducing boredom, promoting mental stimulation, and ensuring the monkey's overall well-being. Budgeting for continual enrichment items such as toys, puzzles, climbing structures, and sensory enrichment helps monkeys maintain their normal habits while reducing stress associated with imprisonment.

- Behavioral Training

Ongoing training and reinforcement of desired actions are critical for controlling the monkey's behavior, dealing with new challenges, and building the link between the monkey and its owner. Budgeting for training sessions, supplies, and prospective expert support helps to maintain constant communication and positive reinforcement approaches.

Legal and Regulatory Compliance

- Permit and Renewal Fees

Compliance with local, state, and federal regulations governing Capuchin monkey ownership requires annual permit or license fees, renewal expenses, and possibly inspection fees. Budgeting for these fees guarantees legal compliance, avoids penalties and fines, and promotes responsible primate ownership.

- Legal Consultation

To negotiate complex regulatory frameworks, handle legal concerns, and maintain compliance with shifting standards, it may be important to consult with legal professionals who are familiar with exotic animal ownership regulations. Budgeting for legal consultation fees clarifies the rights, obligations, and legal safeguards involved with capuchin monkey ownership.

Owning a Capuchin monkey necessitates a significant financial investment to ensure the animal's health, well-being, and legal compliance. From initial purchasing fees and cage setup to ongoing expenses for housing, feeding, veterinary care, and enrichment, potential owners must budget wisely and prepare for long-term financial stability. Understanding the financial ramifications of Capuchin monkey ownership enables people to make informed decisions, give the best care possible, and cultivate a pleasant and meaningful relationship with their primate friend. By emphasizing financial preparedness and good ownership practices, owners can foster a supportive environment that improves the monkey's physical, mental, and emotional health throughout its life.

Chapter 6

Ethical and Welfare Concerns About Keeping Capuchin Monkeys as Pets

Owning a Capuchin monkey as a pet poses substantial ethical and welfare concerns, which must be thoroughly investigated and addressed. These considerations include the monkey's welfare, the ethical implications of confinement and domestication, and the overall impact on conservation efforts and public awareness.

Welfare Considerations

Capuchin monkeys are extremely intelligent, sociable creatures with intricate physical, behavioral, and psychological requirements. Meeting these requirements in captivity necessitates painstaking care, specialized knowledge, and resources to assure their well-being and quality of life.

Physical Needs

- Housing and space requirements

Providing proper shelter is critical for the monkey's physical health and behavioral development. Capuchin monkeys require large cages with climbing structures, perches, and enrichment items that resemble their natural environment. Insufficient space can cause stress, bodily problems, and behavioral concerns.

- Nutrition & Diet

A well-balanced meal that matches the monkey's nutritional needs is critical to their health and longevity. Capuchin monkeys eat a range of fruits, vegetables, proteins, and specialized primate chow. Malnutrition or an inappropriate diet can cause developmental difficulties, metabolic problems, and impaired immunological function.

- Veterinary Care

Access to skilled veterinary care, particularly from doctors who specialize in primate medicine, is crucial for monitoring health, identifying ailments, and delivering timely treatment. Regular health screenings, immunizations, and preventative treatment help to reduce health risks and ensure early intervention for medical problems.

Behavioral Needs

- Socialization and Enrichment

Capuchin monkeys are extremely social animals that flourish in groups with intricate social structures. In captivity, allowing opportunities for socialization with conspecifics or adequate human interaction is critical for their mental and emotional well. Puzzles, toys, and foraging opportunities are examples of enrichment activities that enhance natural behaviors while preventing boredom.

- Cognitive stimulation

Stimulating the monkey's cognitive capacities with problem-solving tasks, training exercises, and environmental enrichment increases mental health and inhibits stereotyping. Cognitive stimulation is essential for preserving their innate intelligence and curiosity.

Psychological Needs

- Stress Management

Reducing stresses and creating a predictable environment are critical for lowering anxiety and boosting psychological well-being. Routine changes, environmental disturbances, or social isolation can all cause stress in Capuchin monkeys, resulting in behavioral disorders and health problems.

- Behavioral Training and Management

Positive reinforcement training strategies serve to manage behavior, promote desired behaviors, and build trust between the monkey and its caregivers. Training sessions should center on fostering healthy relationships, encouraging cooperation, and addressing behavioral issues in humane ways.

Ethical Considerations for Keeping Capuchin Monkeys as Pets

The ethical implications of owning Capuchin monkeys as pets include broader issues such as animal welfare, conservation, and responsible management. These concerns illustrate the complexities and obligations associated with caring for non-human primates in captivity.

Conservation Impact

- Threats to wild populations.

Capuchin monkeys captured from the wild for the exotic pet trade pose a severe danger to natural populations. Habitat destruction, poaching, and illicit wildlife trafficking all contribute to the decline of species populations in their natural environments. Supporting conservation activities and advocating for sustainable practices is critical to protecting natural populations from exploitation.

- Role in Conservation Education

Educating the public on the natural history, conservation status, and ecological significance of capuchin monkeys raises awareness and encourages conservation stewardship. Responsible ownership methods, ethical concerns, and sustainable lifestyles can all help wildlife conservation initiatives.

Welfare Concerns

- Ethical use of animals

The ethical usage of Capuchin monkeys in captivity raises concerns regarding their inherent worth, rights, and ethical treatment. Balancing human goals with the welfare of individual animals necessitates ethical considerations, respect for natural behaviors, and commitment to animal welfare norms.

- Animal Sentience and Cognitive Abilities

Recognizing Capuchin monkeys' sentience and cognitive capacities highlights their ability to experience emotions, form social bonds, and perform complicated activities. Animal welfare-focused ethical frameworks advocate for surroundings that encourage natural behavior, reduce stress, and promote physical and psychological health.

Legal and regulatory frameworks

- Laws and Regulations

The legal systems governing the ownership, trading, and conservation of Capuchin monkeys differ globally and locally. Compliance with local laws, permits, and licensing requirements fosters responsible ownership, raises animal welfare standards, and deters unlawful trafficking and exploitation.

- Enforcement and Compliance

Effective implementation of wildlife protection laws and regulations is critical for combatting illegal trafficking, preserving endangered species, and maintaining ethical animal welfare standards. Collaboration among governmental authorities, conservation organizations, and law enforcement agencies is vital to combating wildlife crime and ensuring legal compliance.

Responsible ownership practices

Promoting appropriate ownership practices entails lobbying for ethical issues, supporting conservation measures, and promoting the welfare of Capuchin monkeys in captivity. Owners and caretakers can help to ensure the well-being of individual monkeys and the survival of their species by following ethical rules, supporting conservation efforts, and campaigning for humane treatment.

Keeping a Capuchin monkey as a pet necessitates navigating difficult ethical considerations and addressing welfare problems to guarantee that their bodily, behavioral, and psychological requirements are addressed. By prioritizing animal welfare, supporting appropriate ownership practices, and advocating for conservation stewardship, owners can provide a healthy and enriching environment for Capuchin monkeys in captivity. Ethical frameworks that acknowledge their intrinsic value, cognitive capacities, and social behaviors inform judgments about their care, treatment, and role in conservation efforts. Individuals can help to improve the welfare and conservation of Capuchin monkeys by advocating responsible stewardship and ethical considerations in exotic animal ownership.

Chapter 7

Alternatives to Capuchin Monkey as Pets

When considering alternatives to Capuchin monkeys as pets, look at other exotic pet possibilities as well as adoption or rescue chances. This section investigates numerous alternative pets as well as the issues surrounding adoption and rescue, providing insights into responsible ownership and ethical considerations.

Other Exotic Pets

Choosing an exotic pet necessitates careful consideration of the animal's needs, compatibility with the owner's lifestyle, and legal obligations. Alternative exotic pets have distinct qualities and behaviors, and each need special care and attention to maintain their well-being.

Exotic Birds

- Parrots and macaws

Parrots and macaws are prominent exotic bird species recognized for their intelligence, vocal talents, and colorful plumage. They require large aviaries or cages, mental stimulation from toys and social interaction, and a healthy diet rich in fruits, vegetables, and seeds. Owners should anticipate extended lifespans and the necessity for ongoing socialization and training.

- Exotic Reptiles

Snakes, lizards, and turtles are intriguing exotic pets that require specific habitats, heating, and lighting. They have specific food requirements, which range from insects and tiny rodents to plant stuff and aquatic species. Proper husbandry, environmental enrichment, and veterinary treatment are critical to their health and well-being.

Small mammals

- Sugar gliders

Sugar gliders are tiny marsupials recognized for their gliding abilities and gregarious behavior. They need big cages with vertical space, specialized meals of fruits, insects, and nectar, and friendship from conspecifics or human caregivers. Bonding through handling and engaging play is critical for their socialization and intellectual stimulation.

- Ferrets

Ferrets are lively and curious little mammals who need large enclosures with many levels for exploration and exercise. They thrive on social connection with humans and other ferrets, a high-protein and fat diet, and mental stimulation from toys and enrichment activities. Routine veterinary care and vaccines are critical to their wellbeing.

Aquatic Pets

- Fish and aquatic invertebrates

Fish and aquatic invertebrates provide a peaceful and low-maintenance option for exotic pet owners. They require aquarium settings that include proper filtration, water quality control, and species-specific foods. Aquascaping and giving hiding places improve their surroundings, encouraging natural behaviors and attractiveness in the home.

- Amphibians

Amphibians, such as frogs and salamanders, make fascinating exotic pets that require amphibian-safe habitats, humidity management, and a varied diet of insects, tiny invertebrates, and plant matter. Maintaining appropriate environmental conditions, such as temperature and moisture levels, helps them meet their health and physiological needs.

- Adoption and Rescue Options

Exploring adoption and rescue alternatives allows you to provide a home for animals in need while also encouraging responsible pet ownership and ethical practices. Adopting from recognized rescue organizations or shelters assures animal wellbeing while also supporting conservation efforts.

Exotic Animal Rescues

- Rescue Organizations

Exotic animal rescue groups focus on the rehabilitation and rehoming of surrendered, abandoned, or seized exotic pets. They offer veterinary treatment, behavioral assessments, and socialization to prepare animals for adoption into suitable homes. Supporting rescue organizations encourages ethical adoption practices while decreasing the demand for wild-caught or commercially bred exotic pets.

- Shelters and sanctuaries

Animal shelters and sanctuaries may occasionally harbor exotic pets that need to be rehomed. These facilities offer interim care, medical treatment, and behavioral rehabilitation to animals before placing them in permanent homes. Adopting from shelters promotes animal welfare and gives animals in need a second opportunity.

Considerations for Adoption

- Species-specific needs

Before adopting an exotic pet, it is critical to understand the species' individual needs, characteristics, and lifespan. Prospective owners can be better prepared for responsible care and long-term commitment by researching their dietary preferences, habitat requirements, socialization needs, and potential health concerns.

- Legal and ethical considerations

Compliance with municipal and federal legislation governing exotic pet ownership is critical for avoiding legal penalties and promoting ethical stewardship. Adopting from reliable providers that encourage animal care, conservation, and appropriate ownership practices reinforces ethical considerations when adopting exotic pets.

Responsible ownership practices

Promoting appropriate ownership practices entails putting animal welfare first, understanding the special needs of exotic pets, and advocating for conservation and ethical stewardship. By giving appropriate care, socialization, and veterinary attention, owners contribute to their pets' well-being and promote sustainable practices in exotic pet ownership.

When looking for alternatives to Capuchin monkeys as pets, you should examine other exotic pet options as well as adoption or rescue chances. Each alternative pet species has distinct qualities, care needs, and considerations for responsible ownership. When selecting an exotic bird, small mammal, aquatic pet, or looking into adoption and rescue alternatives, prioritizing animal welfare, ethical considerations, and legal compliance ensures a good and gratifying experience for both the pet and its owner. Responsible ownership practices, including suitable housing, correct diet, veterinary treatment, and socialization, benefit the health and well-being of exotic pets while encouraging conservation and ethical stewardship within the exotic pet community. Individuals can help to ensure the long-term and compassionate treatment of exotic animals in captivity by making informed decisions and advocating ethical adoption procedures.

Chapter 8

FAQs: Capuchin Monkeys as Pets

1. What is it like to have Capuchin monkeys as pets?

Capuchin monkeys are highly intelligent, sociable primates recognized for their curiosity and dexterity. Pets require substantial care and enrichment to flourish. They form strong bonds with their owners, but they also require interaction with conspecifics or suitable replacements to meet their social demands.

2. Are capuchin monkeys permissible to have as pets?

The legality of possessing capuchin monkeys varies by location. Because of their classification as exotic animals, they are often required to get special permissions or licensing. It is critical to research local legislation and secure the relevant permits to ensure legal compliance.

3. What type of enclosure do Capuchin monkeys require?

Capuchin monkeys require large, secure habitats that imitate their natural habitat. This includes climbing structures, perches, and enrichment items that promote their physical and mental health. Indoor and outdoor access, weather protection, and predator safety are all important factors to consider.

4. What do capuchin monkeys eat?

Their food includes a range of fruits, vegetables, nuts, seeds, and protein sources like as insects and small animals. Commercial monkey chow tailored to their nutritional requirements may also be part of their diet. A balanced diet is essential for preventing nutritional deficits.

5. Do Capuchin monkeys require specialized veterinarian care?

Yes, Capuchin monkeys require frequent veterinarian examinations by professionals trained in primate medicine. They may require vaccines, parasite control, dental care, and treatment for specific health issues. Early detection and treatment of health problems is crucial to their well-being.

6. How can you socialize a Capuchin monkey?

Socialization is essential for Capuchin monkeys to establish appropriate behavior and form bonds with their caregivers. Positive interactions with people, as well as opportunities to connect with conspecifics or other appropriate animals, help to improve social skills and prevent behavioral issues.

7. Are the Capuchin monkeys aggressive?

Capuchin monkeys, like any other species, can be aggressive, particularly when attacked or agitated. Proper socializing, positive reinforcement training, and understanding their body language can all assist manage their behavior and reduce violence.

8. What are the ethical considerations while keeping Capuchin monkeys as pets?

Owning a capuchin monkey raises ethical problems concerning their welfare, conservation, and the legality of exotic pet ownership. To maintain responsible ownership, it is critical to emphasize their well-being, understand their natural habits, and follow all applicable regulations.

9. How long do capuchin monkeys live?

Capuchin monkeys can live for 25 to 40 years or more in captivity, depending on their health, nutrition, and living conditions. When thinking about them as pets, you must be committed to their care and well-being for the long term.

10. Can capuchin monkeys be trained?

Yes, Capuchin monkeys can be trained to do a range of activities using positive reinforcement approaches. Basic commands, social behaviors, and cognitive challenges can all be used to activate their innate skills throughout training.

11. What are the challenges of owning a Capuchin monkey?

Their extended lifetime, unique care requirements, legal considerations, and the need for comprehensive enrichment all pose challenges. Owners must also budget for the financial expenses involved with their care, such as veterinarian bills and housing.

12. How much does it cost to possess a capuchin monkey?

The costs vary greatly depending on aspects including procurement, cage setup, ongoing maintenance, and veterinarian bills. The initial charges can range from several thousand to tens of thousands of dollars, with further expenses for food, enrichment, and healthcare.

13. Where can I adopt or buy a Capuchin monkey?

Capuchin monkeys can be obtained via trustworthy breeders, exotic animal rescues, or individuals who want to rehome their pets. It is critical to thoroughly examine the source, ensuring that they follow ethical standards and legal criteria.

14. What should I consider before purchasing a Capuchin monkey?

Before adopting a Capuchin monkey, examine your capacity to meet their complicated requirements, which include space, time commitment, financial resources, and legal duties. Research their care needs extensively and be prepared to make a long-term commitment to their well-being.

15. How can I ensure the well-being of a Capuchin monkey in captivity?

A Capuchin monkey's welfare is ensured by providing a stimulating habitat, sufficient nourishment, veterinary treatment, socializing, and enrichment activities. Understanding their natural behaviors and requirements is critical to improving their physical, mental, and emotional wellbeing.

Understanding the responsibilities and considerations of keeping a Capuchin monkey as a pet is essential for making sound decisions. These FAQs address common questions and concerns, allowing potential owners to better prepare for the challenges and joys of caring for these clever and social monkeys. Prioritizing their care, legal compliance, and ethical considerations promotes a healthy and rewarding interaction between people and capuchin monkeys in captivity.

Conclusion

The conclusion presents a complete summary of significant themes explored throughout this investigation into Capuchin monkeys as pets, including their care, ethical considerations, and responsibilities of ownership. It also includes closing comments and recommendations for prospective owners to guarantee the welfare of these clever and social primates in captivity.

Summary of Key Points:

Throughout this debate, several important aspects of owning Capuchin monkeys as pets have been highlighted:

Capuchin monkeys require specific care, such as large cages with enrichment, a balanced food, frequent veterinarian check-ups, and socialization, to ensure their physical and mental health.

Legal and ethical considerations: The legality of keeping Capuchin monkeys varies by location and frequently necessitates permissions or licenses. Ethical considerations include the wellbeing of captive animals, conservation consequences, and ethical stewardship.

Behavior & Training: Understanding Capuchin monkeys' natural tendencies and adopting positive reinforcement training methods are critical for regulating their behavior and building a bond with caregivers.

Costs and Financial Commitments: Ownership entails major financial commitments, such as initial setup fees and ongoing expenses for housing, diet, veterinary care, and enrichment, which necessitate careful budgeting and planning.

Welfare and Ethical problems: Addressing welfare problems entails addressing people's physical, behavioral, and psychological requirements, encouraging ethical ownership practices, and supporting conservation efforts.

Exploring alternative pets and adoption alternatives promotes responsible ownership, ethical considerations, and chances to help animal welfare efforts.

FAQs and Common inquiries: Responding to common inquiries about Capuchin monkeys as pets enables potential owners to make educated decisions and appropriately prepare for the challenges and rewards of ownership.

Final thoughts and recommendations

Owning a Capuchin monkey as a pet is a huge responsibility that demands commitment, expertise, and resources to maintain their safety and legal compliance. Here are some final comments and suggestions for prospective owners:

1. Educate yourself thoroughly.

Before selecting Capuchin monkeys as pets, do extensive research on their care requirements, behavioral characteristics, and local legal constraints. Understanding their needs and duties is critical for providing appropriate care and maintaining a happy living environment.

2. Provide a stimulating environment.

Create an enhanced environment that resembles their natural habitat, complete with climbing structures, enrichment items, and opportunities for social interaction. Mental stimulation, such as puzzles, foraging activities, and training sessions, improves cognitive capacities and eliminates boredom.

3. Commit to proper nutrition and veterinary care.

Maintain a balanced diet that meets their nutritional requirements, including fresh fruits and vegetables, meats, and specialized primate chow. Regular veterinary check-ups, immunizations, and preventive treatment are critical for recognizing and treating health problems early.

4. Promote socialization and positive reinforcement.
Capuchin monkeys thrive on social connection, whether with their conspecifics or human caregivers. Positive reinforcement training fosters trust, rewards desired behaviors, and enhances the monkey's link with its owner. Understanding their communication cues and respecting their boundaries leads to a harmonious connection.

5. Consider the ethical and welfare implications.
Consider the ethical consequences of keeping Capuchin monkeys as pets, such as their wellbeing, environmental impact, and legal duties. Prioritize their well-being, contribute to conservation efforts, and promote appropriate ownership practices within the exotic pet community.

6. Plan financially for long-term care.
Plan for initial setup costs, ongoing expenses for housing, diet, veterinary care, and unforeseen crises. Financial readiness

guarantees that you can give ongoing care and fulfill their changing demands throughout their lives.

7. Investigate Adoption and Rescue Opportunities.
Consider adopting from a reputable rescue group or shelter that values animal care and conservation. Adopting gives animals in need a second opportunity and helps to minimize the demand for exotic pets that have been caught wild or produced commercially.

8. Advocate for responsible ownership.
Encourage appropriate ownership practices by educating others on the difficulties of exotic pet ownership, advocating for ethical issues, and supporting projects that prioritize animal welfare and conservation management.

Keeping a Capuchin monkey as a pet necessitates careful consideration of their complicated demands, legal obligations, and ethical consequences. Owners may ensure that these cognitive primates in captivity live full and enriching lives by prioritizing their wellbeing, giving proper care, and maintaining a good atmosphere. Individuals may help Capuchin monkeys by providing information, responsible stewardship, and ethical participation. They can also support sustainable practices in exotic pet ownership. Making informed judgments and accepting ownership duties are critical steps in creating a supportive and empathetic environment in which Capuchin monkeys can be treasured companions in responsible and aware homes.